Three Musicians

ROD TOWNLEY

Drawings by Wendy Edelson

THE SMITH

by arrangement with Horizon Press

New York   1978

ACKNOWLEDGMENTS

Various poems in this collection were awarded first prize in college contests sponsored by The Academy of American Poets in 1969 and again in 1971.

"The Furnished Field" appeared in the anthology *University and College Poetry Prizes 1967-72*, edited by Daniel Hoffman, The Academy of American Poets, 1974. "Pieta" appeared in the anthology *Eleven Young Poets*, edited by Ray Boxer, The Smith, 1975.

"Summer Street" was first published as a separate pamphlet by The Smith, 1976. "June 1942" was printed as a broadside by Philadelphia '76, Inc., 1976.

In addition, a number of poems have appeared in magazines: "Omelet Vision," "Vigil," and "Swimmer" in *The Village Voice;* "Forgetting," "Dedication," and "Plain-Chant" in *U.S. 1;* "The Bait" in *The Smith;* "A Devotion for Travelers" and "Last Will" in *Fragments;* "Bestiary" in *Stone Drum;* and "New Jersey Turnpike" in *Today (The Philadelphia Inquirer's* Sunday magazine).

Note: In 1972 a privately printed booklet appeared, without copyright, entitled *Blue Angels Black Angels*. The present volume retains (often in greatly revised form) a few poems from that work and adds many poems written since that time.

First Edition

Library of Congress Catalog Number: 77-82686

ISBN: 0-912292-43-1

English (change)

Contents

This book is for Libby Blackman

Crois-tu qu'il est si simple
de se débarrasser d'une blessure,
de fermer la bouche d'une blessure?
— Cocteau

I

Pieta

(for Gil Orlovitz)

A hammer to the face.
        Rebuild at once.

The leaf on the final twig
of the redwood shudders,
the first blow of the ax
into the juice,
the thud in the heart,
the upward flood of time
bleeding out:

Be worthy of the next assassin.

Throw it against the wall.
It returns
        with stinging force
                numbing the hand.

In a time of dream
        at a sound
like the sound of wings look up —

Steel and stone exchange
rough caresses

        *

Superb man

        Your beauty

             Your

crushed broken-nosed face knew
all loveliness comes at last
to the hammer.

I'm tired
I'm 472 years older than
you at my age and your Pieta which today

9

Old man
I commission your next work, see it is done
in my house. My hands are yours,
strong arms, blooded brain, eyes.

You have the run of me.

*

I go up to the mountain trembling
and weaponless. Against America
my hand is the forefoot of an ant.
What shape shall I caress the continent?

I approach slowly, looking for mirrors,
and find the footpaths paved, blades spinning
where trees once roared. Fear
is the last gas station before the summit.

I continue on foot; find a violet
and do not pick it; a wounded woodchuck
and stroke it till it sleeps; a sunfish
left gasping, slip it into a lake

hoping I am in the world of myth.

*

It is summer. The wet snows
of March have sunk in the ground
and risen in the trees. The white
apple blossoms have fallen
into daisies and queen anne's lace
rising beneath them, whiteness
renewing itself like foam
upon green waves.

Earth knows about death.
In the summer of blood and honey
no one is safe. The cat his bright claw.
the fish the flash of teeth,
and men to the white marble
give their trust. But in a season
they all are lost. Ice breaks.
A hammer cracks the stone.

*

The children's voices die out of the woods.
A moment of stillness
and then the wind
slowly sweeps the trees
announcing the approach of the spirit.

Beneath leather
my legs are motionless
as the white-stemmed
indian pipes in the leafy mulch
beside the river.

I cease to exist
as the wind resumes
hustling over the leaves
finding everything
and slowly
the foot of the doe lowers
and birds return
and the fly on the sunny stone
becomes perfect, and once more
the poem begins its approach
through the woods
like some hidden misery

Part One

*"While beauty burned . . . death and
torment both seemed exquisite."*
1548

The old man's hand,
most perfect instrument of touch
since Christ, now crooked sticks, ruined,
loosens its grip on the sheet
as the eyes close
and he sees

the tormenting image
blazed in sonnets he wrote as a boy
and destroyed, showing
not even Lorenzo:

        (a young woman . . .
                  (Nike?
                            (naked by the sea . . .
"Racing the foam and wind and bleating gull,
Her heart a rage within her, her mind a torrent . . ."

Five centuries later she is riding
a bus into Philadelphia
her mouth pursed open
as if about to say
wonderful.

        rock   nude   sky

The green-tinged window
throws her into a dream
in which she sees herself
running,
wearing the wind.
Each blink of her eyes
in the stinging air returns her
like shells
into the slippery sea.

       *

Beauty is the great catastrophe,
drives us to the rocks.

        "Don't tell them how
        you found me"—the drunk
        with glass in his meticulous hands.

It is beauty holds the knife
to the ribs, saying Go on.

        He woke among the flowers of Redon,
        found two weeping spiders
        dangling at the end of his arms.

In the available light
of a telephone booth
on a dark street
a fat boy
opens the September issue
to the center.

It is the same
agony of line
made Michelangelo wince,
the perfect nude
flashing through the city.
For there are moods
the mind knows nothing of,
as when the bone
surfaces like a brook
at the hip
which flesh mitigates
into a highly
sophisticated smile
angling to the crotch;

as when the young girlbelly pouts
in sullen exaggeration
of an imagined wrong;
as when the hand
sleeps in a hand,
careless of intimacy;

as when in dream
the feet are severed
and join
the stupid mastodons
in humorless bliss;

as when the woman's arm
joins her side
like a sleek animal
its mother, and takes
the caress for granted,
as when

the breast awakens
a mild blind eye to the world
it knows by touch,
the pure human trajectory
of outward,
a stone's throw,
impertinance
against the pull of time
is its perfection.

Coda

All toys have the right to break,
said Antonio Porchia, dying,
an escape upward to form
and a return
that follows the gaze
of the stone madonna,
Lady of the Rocks.

The fountain leaps up,
the pure hieroglyph
written in water on the air,
and dies back in itself
whispering
of the greatness of surrender.

Christ is dead his
blood spilled and the mother at the
moment of focussed perfection has
begun looking down

Part Two

*"I work and suffer more than
anybody ever did; I am not well
and I work hard." 1512*

Accept one gift from the enemy
and you are no hero.

Watching the ribbed sand
under the escaping wave
like a firm tanned body
a sheet is pulled from, it seems
easy to be naked and to write
poems time will erase,
patterns that will shift
into someone else's words about the sea.

Not to be stone, not to be set
to explode in rage
at every breath the sea takes,

but to be flesh, but to let
water pull the clothing from you,
set free the hair,
set free the gesturing arms
to float like bread on the waters.

That, or hack the rock
into slaves that will serve you forever.

    *

Now is the time,
under the threat of blows,
the easel flailing in the windy cornfield

A century ago
Van Gogh blew out

his brains, his blood was too late
to help the crop.

Reduced to powder, gathered,
it explodes in the palette of Vlaminck.

Gather bits of stone from the Vatican floor.

White
the conflagration, the force

reverses the footage from Hue
so it ends alive.

Pale faces of the dead
begin to feel the sun

now, while the wind increases
and not even crows are left
and dead stalks bark their shins.

Wild men have lived in these woods, men with eyes
lidless to the moon, ready to catch fire
         sky

     nude

  rock

the clouds move fast over the land, even now
with enough speed the world returns to the world,

black blizzards of trees fly past
each tree a man, each wilderness

a sea of arms outspread against the velocity of numbers,
at night

the groves of oak permitted by the Highway Authority
bulge forward like smoke

catch headlights in a net of twigs
then loom off. Wild men live here

turned into trees,
bony twigs jabbing the moon, men

not to be housed in rows
of bungalows spilling with light, men

in the employ of winter, crazed deserters
from all the armies

climb
from the mud-slicked trenches.

Coda

Prayer spoken at La Cathédrale
de Notre Dame de Bruges
while crossing George Washington
Bridge Christmas week
the text lost like smoke
mingling in mist, headlights
in mid-afternoon, curved steel
rising and dissolving
like a memory of the present,
the past a vaulted door
the mind has entered thinking
America is roofless and unconsecrated,
not like the past
where a white marble madonna,

sister to the one destroyed,
presides over our prayers.

We come here, madmen in love,
to stand at the back at vespers
gazing across rows of bowed shoulders
past festooned candles
and white calendula to her face,
flesh in the quilted light,
sweetness and strength
no longer Michelangelo's, hers now,
radiant, and ours
who reach across the space of time,
rivers of petitioners and
drive across,
while the bridge dissolves behind us.

Part Three

"Be patient, everywhere there is
more grief than you imagine."
                    1515

There was no photograph of midnight canals
or of the swans floating asleep in the dark.
Though he shook book after book from the freezing attic
no photograph fell of her sleeping face
in a golden tent above Florence; no

photograph of olive trees at Lago
di Garda, silver in the rain-turning wind
where she swam in choppy waves and left
ahead of news reports and fatal mudslides.

Though he pored through boxes of letters there was
no photograph of a summer evening downpour
in Paris, their faces flushed with wine and defiance
as they raced the length of la Rue de Varenne
to a room where, again, they did not dare touch.

His hand trembled with cold but found no photograph
of the tarnished cornfield where he waited,

17

no photograph of her set face driving
through rain to Oostende, no photograph
of his flinging her shoes into the waves,
nor of her laugh, nor of their hands resting together
at a great distance and for the last time perfect
as marble worked by a master almost to flesh,
almost to move, and grip, and not let go.

                    *

You see them lying under cliffs by the ocean,
boulders stripped of earth,
great carcasses
holding nothing up or down.

At your home in town
envelopes arrive in desperate straits,
urgent requests, torn sleeves,
the heart racing out at the wrist.

A white blizzard laced red
the letters pour in filling the vestibule:
poets who've sold their signatures
write for loans;

painters scrawl from the safety of their binges;
a woman with one warm and one cool vein
writes of white afternoons
and the sound of bone china.

You stare out windows
at the first snowfall. The mailman
slants against the hill. All
afternoon no let-up.

Packages arrive from war zones
in stiff gauze,
Cambodian pillows burst open
in a flurry of postcards:

Angkor Wat with reindeer,
Angkor Wat with soldiers,
the Imperial Palace,
aerial view.

Through the heat ducts
smells of the dying landlady rise
to every room of the house.

Coda

The boulders by the sea are buried.
Snow drives down on them.
He stands
in soft shadows and looks out.
The snow drives down.
He looks at it falling on the water
while light lowers
and flakes cannot be told
one from another
as they race into the black troughs
of the sea. And he is close,
and knows it, and begins
forgetting as shadows dissolve in the dusk,
as earth, stone, ocean
dissolve in the dusk; the
air swirls; invisible snow
dies in invisible seas; the eye
deceives him, the ear
plays him false in the bannered wind,
senses disintegrate in a
disappearing landscape. All is air
but close as a cloister,
all is sky, the naked rock
clothed in it, but the planetarium
is shut for the night.
In his dream all the statues
have been set out by the shore
to be healed; they face out
to watch as the ships
sailing from Carrara founder
and the great blocks,
as slowly as snow, sink
down for the sea to inscribe
like coral; and snow
falls into the ocean

and statues forget their limbs
and their perfect features
blur into ice, build
back into cliffsides. The world
grows to a burial mound.
Origin, existence, disappearance are
all one. Snow
drives down on land's end,
relieved of us, sealed
in the bountiful dark.

Shadow

The shore of drunkenness is
smooth as a girl.
No one comes here.

Waves file in
bearing pieces of the night
and then withdraw

and night like a statue
assembles itself
before your eyes.

Light up your pipes
seraphim,
sit back and leak
no twilight.

Dedication

For Anna, young girl, freedom and fear
in the ocarinas of the summer night,
for Anna Akhmatova who stood in line
when youth was gone and the Russia
of her youth was gone, her men
gunned down by the goons of obedience
while she waited by the flagrant wall
for word, for the poet Akhmatova
to whom words came like black doves
flying over the prison by the Neva

Talisman

(for Muriel Rukeyser)

Forced to a standstill by a double R
that stops for no man I write your name
Muriel as talisman and try
for a poem. Warding off the wait, the
dead time underground. I need

your work. To speak at all, in what moments
are grudged us between orders
to move on. Cramped, insulted, inconvenient
our lives, yet your lines
new-minted leaves spread forth in such
generosity you'd think —

But the train I was
angry to miss comes on now
like a curse. My fingers shake.
No time to think
of the place you've fought your way
through to. I thrust my hands
in my pockets and go on.

Swimmer

(for Katherine Houghton)

That lean-years look made me smile,
I'm that perverse, as you spoke
to what part of the nation was awake
for the Today Show of the artist's life.

The great vat of American cream cheese
you surfaced from, lank individualist,
closed over you for a Tide commercial
while you pled for federal subsidies.

Dive down, swimmer. With a small knife
do what work you must. The artist
is saboteur of sleep. Expect nothing
from a blind land that has designs on your eyes.

The Bait

Slowly
as though blessing the waters
the hand moves.

With no
more sound than an insect makes
when its foot-

ing in
air is lost, the bait
is placed.

The line
lies motionless. It blends
with water.

In a tuft
of hair and a single false
feather rides

the gold hook.

The Dry Moon

(for Gil Orlovitz)

For a
torrential man in a dry time
the booze of hope keeping
a pendant penis wagging
across the page in search
of the lost mother whose trail
drips off in the dark under the
rumbling El

there are still
a thousand and one nights
to piss away, a hundred black ribbons
to hang above the arena
of a borrowed typewriter, a dozen joys
snailing across cobblestones
in the run-down neighborhoods
of evening.

Rachmaninoff
never hauled pianos up narrower
stairwells while under hypnosis
nor drew from the dry moon more
hysterical seascapes for men
to toil on and be told, "You are
falling asleep, you are falling
asleep . . ."

Half a century
without the dark slake of Eve
taking what wet you can
from a thirsty world, do not expect
me to wipe seepage from dead eyes.
I will labor only on proofs
of your mortality or immortality, torrential man
in this dry time.

II

Forgetting

The cheekbones, delicately cushioned,
are what you touch first
to be sure of the girl's mortality.

Established. You begin
rummaging through her beauty
as through belongings, looking for

you forget what.

Vigil

I kept a vigil the snowy night
you left over the body of a sleeping child
(a cough hooked in his throat tugging him up,
letting him drop back deep, his body stranded
on the twisted sheets); I stroked
his back, thought of your long legs
twisting around another man's body
in the throes of farewell, sopping urchins
cramming the last bit in before the long fast
to the coast. You were magnificent.
The boy becalmed slipped free of both of us,
no anger of mine to choke on, to that final floor
of the unborn where, swallowing our fears,
we are all each other's perfect meat.

Lost

They throw everything at us at once—cars,
dogs, skies, women, fill in the blanks,
and among them a face, yours, scathed
with too much sorting through, forced to
refuse image after image, plate glass,
sunlight glazing a roof, my daunted eyes
looking at you covertly from the relative
safety of fatherhood, my child my shield
from the blue inquisition of your glance.
And now it is autumn they send down on us,
bewildering leaves, wet walks, and always the child
between us keeping our hands at one remove
from the imbecilities of passion, as if to prove
there's no way through this . . . .

The Wounds

Sylla bedeck me— she

bit her lip till
it bled
and held me to it. I

        could not tell, I, breathless, where
                wound ended and kiss began but I know
                (winter afflict) I led her

      took Corinne

            sang

        "Sleep your face off
        your breast
        awake in my hand"

Erros occur.
      Stars are
smeared from the slate. Begin again, a

          chill air, a
       deck of a bed
            lust cribbed us

     tongue-lashed in
        the place of deception
            (even the moon

        was taken in,
        hung like a mirror
        over her cheap perfumes.)

Air is a girl. With

        blood-daubed fingers I traced
        the shadow's bone. I could see

          her move,
                    her forehead
                         hammered the air, I could see

     her moving above me in the darkness a lioness
     at a private feast

Visiting Friends

(for C.D.)

Afternoon and a strange calmness.
Your room is empty.
Quietly I go through your bureau
looking for things that know you.

Pat comes in with the crossword
puzzle, stares, says nothing. Does
he think I'm stealing from him?

*

They looked at me
but let me in when they saw your mink.
Pat was paying and was sober
but we were smashed. A dozen
thin gold necklaces
lay over your breasts
like a bondage and I wondered
how you would look in chains.
Pat talked about Taiwan and where
he had taken you and I wondered
if he had given you
those necklaces all in a heap
or singly,
country by country,
house by garden,
stock by bond.

*

You inform me he disapproves
of drugs, then drug him. While
he sleeps you sit on the zebra
before the fire and roll joints.

He walks in, wants to know
what the smell is. "I
burned the rug."
"The zebra? God no, where?"
"It's all right. You can't see
it. It's on one of the stripes."

*

In a corner of the attic
an electric heater
looks on intently
making our bodies glow,
throws us to blackness
every three minutes
like a warning,
then three minutes
flushes warm.

Which way is lovelier?
No need to decide.
I love you when I see you,
your breasts amber
in the strange light, eyes
of moth wings and I love you
in your absence
to all sense but one.

Propping myself on an elbow
I stroke your cheek, complacent
as Central Park. The heat
clicks on and I see, dizzy
as I am, your smile
run rings around me.

A Devotion for Travelers

(for Wheeler Dixon)

There is a safety in night.
For half a minute I cut
my lights and feel the sharpness
of stars on all sides
and pointless earth, and I think
for no reason of Br'er Rabbit
flinging from the cliff to certain death
and landing instead
feet-first in secrecy.
Night is like that.
Lethal to most it is
my briarpatch, a test
which only the helpless pass
whose brains are small furred
animals racing
through the subconscious of Oklahoma
at 75 with the lights off.
Try it sometime, girl,
when you are feeling
sure of your beauty.

Volen: A Novel

(for J.D.)

Composition

On your imperfect beauty I will build,
Volen thought, noting the caramel smile
of her belly as she
stretched backwards in her chair.

He drew red pencils
through her love poems
to someone else, through the line
"My nude fragile body trembled in the dark."

Later That Night

That mouth, that gross contraption
slung together on a slack string, those
rough-looking lips yanked back
from the teeth
into a meat-eater smile by
tough quotation-mark muscles,
cheekbones, jawbone

forced their way through his dream
like a fist, his stomach hurting,
his eyes in the dark room grown
into blades of grass like a cat's
in a mad corner of the garden.

His Fear of Whiteness

Rubber slickers, wet whips
coffee brandy afternoons
a smear of oil on her neck,

his heart started
like a car, she looked out
the attic window

at a white gull sailing through the rain.

His Dream

The smell of honeysuckle
along the highway called up from dream
her mussed and covetous eyes

wild as an animal's faced
with its desire, her long red hair
tangled with shit as she knelt

naked on the tile floor.

The Last Letter

"I want no photograph.
I won't have you
breathed over with the yellow breath
of the animal that lives
by my door on what I toss him
to keep his mind off my throat.
And I would toss him you.

"Come only in dream
if at all. You won't then pass
the narrow place where my hands
must have at you
like an avalanche committing a village
to memory: street,
doorway, table, drinking cup."

The Polly Poems

Polly Learns A Secret

White tile and silver mirrors tell
Polly a secret in the silent house
as she steps from the shower and sees
(hands loose along slippery thighs)
a full woman watching in the mist.

Polly At The Seashore

Waves breaking on all sides like Tiffany's
gone to smash, she diver in
fearless amid fake dangers, her body
one long ligament twisted taut
as a golden rope, eyes cold as clams.

Polly's Dream Comes True

The dark bucket seat is cool to her
bare thighs; she picks up speed:
her small foot squeezes the pedal
like a trigger; stunned with sunlight
the road wavers through green glass.

The Furnished Field

1.

I was there. Where were you?
Dead asleep, no doubt, beside your husband.

I stole the carpeting, dragged it deep
into the field, the dust
sowed itself in the wet grass. Also a pillow

I found in the attic, heavy with mildew.
Quite a luxury.

I spread it out and
started waiting for you to get the courage.

2.

I listened to that one elm out there
yelling at me, and

I listened to the grass
four feet high at least surrounding me
where I waited, and then

I heard it moving
aside, yessing you the way to me.

I stood up. It was bright as day,
you should have seen it,
the whole field moving in a silver tide.

3.

I lay down again, tried sleeping, but always
the grass would move and

I'd hear your steps.
Today in dead daylight it sounds odd but
I thought you'd come.

I am too simple.
I should have seen through you, should have known
beauty would panic you.

I was there. For me it is
now a poem. What's it for you Mrs. Barbash?

Plain-chant

(for L.B.)

Watching her measure herself
up the stairs like a charwoman
her sheepskin coat and wool cap
still smart despite repairs
always with the wrong thread
and fingers clumsy with anger,
watching the tarnished coat
about and about the stairwell
mounting like a heavy shield
held to five years' dirty weather
and mixed luck, watching her eyes
approaching the landing lift
to mine without reproach and move
past me into the dim rooms

Recovery

After a time-ridden hag
of a day I play
piano, thinking my big hand
is on your little hand.

My heart is not pure.

It was not a river
but a deadline I crossed
to get to the bank.
It was not a lover

but an hour.

At the Flame
playing piano I am recovering
composure. The music is not pure
(I skip beats) but slowly

I come to my senses.

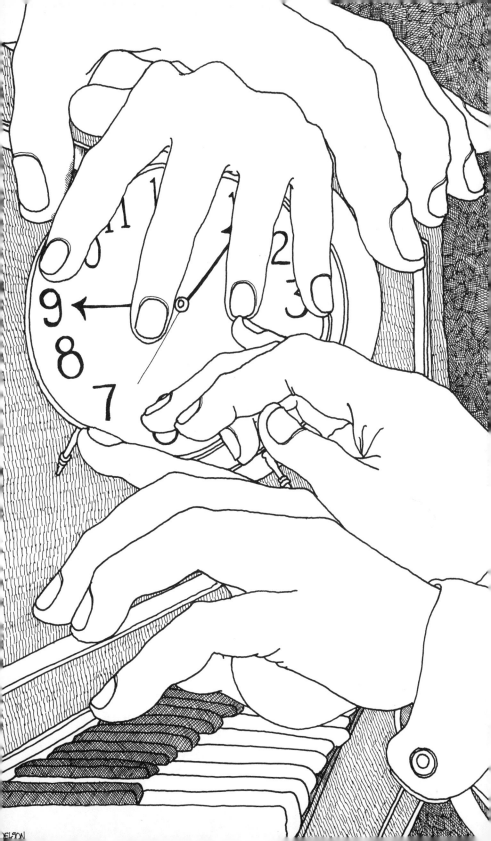

June 1942

The wail of the alert
had just begun and in the dark
the snuffling of the shushed
children under the table

when you threw open the
shutters, went about with
lanterns casting shafts
into the dangerous night. "Kate!

Kate!" we screamed. "Crazy

bitch," said Father, taking
the lights from you
as one would take knives
from a child. The darkness

restored, we looked out.
The distant city
was like a lake of lights. Fires
were breaking out everywhere.

III

Still Life

In the deserted house
in the silent
kitchen, in a white dish
on the white table stands
a perfect pear.

A day later
it is still perfect.

During the week
a small spot forms
like a beauty mark
but it is not
a beauty mark.

Light green, then
light brown, then
wider.

The motionless air
suggests
a sweet smell.
Another week
and there can be no mistake.

The air is a sick nectar.

Still you have not returned.

Near the Highway

Terror is patient in small beasts,
settles about them
comfortably, stroking their fur
gently the wrong way.

New Jersey Turnpike

In the scooped flight of the great bridge,
in the sudden moon
over the silted river mouth, orchid
of black mud, perfection,
and in the smudged line of evening
slanting to oil fields and the winter night,
towers and fires,

and in the greatness of desire,
perfection, and in loss of desire,
the slow modulation to silence
down the spirals of the leaves,
perfection in the healing of wounds,
the closing of earth after us.

The Poetry of Death

Death by statement.

Until the word's reprieve
no one is saved.

.statement by Death

Until the word's reprieve
no one is saved

Therefore the poem

the words climbing
from their cages

among the wreckage

Last Will

do an autopsy
you'll find a spool of film

run it
you'll see a city

see on the left
behind the lights

that dark street
take it

i'll be waiting
at the end of it

with camera & knives

The Last Survivor

from the Anglo-Saxon

"Earth, hold for us, now we no longer can,
our heavy wealth. In the beginning, men
took it from you. Now death has taken them,
war-terror taken every one of my people.
Once they reveled in hall-pleasures, sang
light songs. Now none is left. No one
can lift the sword, polish the plated bowl.
The pitcher lies beside the servant's hand.
Helmets are stripped of plating, shorn
of the difficult gold. Servants sleep
who should burnish the war-masks.
Also the corselet, which in battle staved-off
the bite of metal over the shield's clash,
lies here mouthed by earth like its owner.
Never again will the armor go with him,
cross the sea by the hero's side.
No joy in the harp, delight in timbrel.
No good hawk swings through the hall. No
swift horse stamps in the courtyard. Death
has taken all the race of men."

Sea Burial

(for Sarah Cotterill)

1.
The waves came in all night
and all the next day, the sky
grey as a gull's back

My father's death
took place at impossible distances

the white sheets
his veined
rooty hand resting in mine

I was not there, it was all
some miracle of mirrors

2.
We came, mother and I
lugging our load, a drizzling sunlight
baffled me

Jones Beach deserted
too early in the season for bathers
the water too cold

The wire handle
pulled down like a garrotte
magnetized
to the center of the earth

3.
I pried it open, the can
with no label, no list
of ingredients, but shiny,
shiny!

I stuck a bare fist in,
into that

gravelly stuff, some of it
getting under the fingernails

and flung it —
flung it out into the sea
handful on handful till I thought
there'd be no end to it.

4.
When it was over
I turned from the work
furious

I did not recognize the woman
her dress

flapping like a black flag
in the grey wind

1665

1.

In Spittlefields the Widow Bronson's legs forgot her.
Her eyes grew milky at the sight of tables
laden like her mother's smile
for the prettiest daughter.

2.

In the cart from Newgate to the fatal tree
Moll knew not what the others felt
but for herself she owned
her soul was lethargy.

3.

The maiden learned with sudden, slow surprise
the sweat of sickness. Her mistress
held the candle, saw fatal tokens
on the inside of her thighs.

The Months

January

Elbows on the sill, hot chocolate and
a marshmallow in a white cup, she
stares out at the windless snow, the
disappearing yard, wood chips, the rusting
wheelbarrow and beyond—the grey scarf
that yesterday was a road into town.
If this keeps up, she thinks. She sips at
the steaming drink. Tomorrow will
be skis! A man comes up behind her,
rests his hands gently on her hips.

February

His eyes double-seeded with fire
and with ice fight frozen windshields
crazed snowcrusts (broken under wheels)
toward a house, a country street, dusk.

The girl brushing her hair by candlelight
forgets (eyes warm, abstract) the winter sun
a bare bulb held to the face all afternoon
merciless as light from a billion pearls.

March

Flashing trees, cold hands up for grabs,
foot-races through the slush, another beer,
dancing dancing to the point of closing
the deal, a rush decision, do this or
do that. Driving separate cars home, the
windows unrolled to the rain, wrists wet,
suddenly he calls out across the
loud sluice of darkness her secret name.

April

Incessant trickling, infant death, muck
in the back yard, rents, twigs, blackbirds
shivering on a branch, irreparable spring
advances through the suburbs, the streets
deserted but for an old man in
mackinaw patrolling a corner of
last year. His eyes lift to the black house
narrow and wooden where, the rumors go,
a pale young couple has moved in.

May

An outdoor booksale under volatile skies, a
Dance to the Music of Time, two-fifty and a
chaser of warm rain disarm the man, pay out
a few more paces to his leashed heart. The young
woman heading for cover under the band shell
is not the lover who wandered with open eyes
into his line of sight seasons ago.

June

A violent wedge of sun splits the shadow
of the commuter train like a threshing blade: rocks
daisies, white picket, leaves flash green and
chancy through the ratchets of diamond light. Not

until evening, hauling himself up against
the inclination of a taciturn street
past death-of-a-salesman shadows and
stagey streetlamps does the vision of
morning sunlight desert him.

July

Anything could happen in the night
of barking dogs, the hot night of independence
for the drivers of negroes. Could anything
still happen?
          In a passion of despair
their hands lock, they walk away from
the others. Her white shirt falls open
in a dark corner of the park.

August

Summer frays into tawdry queen anne's lace
under the window where, swollen, slippery with
fear the woman twists bedclothes into
soaked shackles. No! It is not to be
borne, not to be denied. Exhausted air
lies in the room like clear plastic. Not to be
born is best, she thinks, then a cry
no one has heard before tears open the
walls and the wind streams in.

September

About two free animals love's entrapment
is complete. She watches him go in darkness,
return in darkness. From her high window
she sees the days advance, women push and
tug bundles through the town: all the
thick-waisted women, the low slung and
high breasted women, short of life breath
lugging laundry up the tilt of a mighty
September afternoon ten years, twenty years, a
thousand zig-zag miles from here to around the
corner, to a frame house with a view of the park.

October

Falling asleep in afternoon, waking in
panic, he looks out at the thinning
cherry trees for his lost resolution.
Where is her last letter? Already packed.
With the rugs rolled, the house with so many doors
leading from warm room to room turns
suddenly from him. His life and
child on his back, he hires a ride
to the nearest crowded city.

November

The wet wind mucking with the trees behind
a high wall, November's last warm rains
well hung ill wed provoke mad singing
among sparrows in the splashing branches yellow
as the boy's rubber boots which have yet
to miss a homeward puddle, his small fist
twisting his father's sleeve across the street.

December

The flags waver in the frozen light.
A fault appears and is at once published
in the high windows of the office tower.
The wind grows colder. Now there are clouds
and all the mother-of-pearl pageantry of a
winter afternoon. He declines it. Leaving
his cup on the sill he turns back
to the room he has been painting "Country Red."

Riding Home

(for Thor, born August 6, 1939; died August 8, 1957)

Born yesterday, due to die
tomorrow, you are with me
the long drive home. I have spent
days up to my mind in ink.
Death is not far. Mine
is not the only carapace
down-shifting under the moon.

Two nights ago, alone on
the eve of your birth, we met.
All day I had been reading Williams'
letters to his brother Edgar,
the manuscripts brittle
as cicada shells you find
fastened to trees.

That night when I saw you I thought
why have I not
written to you all these years?

       *

In a blurred tree crickets
are screaming secrets
which a second seals off from us,
for I am driving home. Piles
of xeroxed pages think in the back seat.

As a child I knew that somewhere
records are kept, no night is lost, waves
crashing like midnight chandeliers.

But there is only one night and it
has always been lost. Again and again I see
your impassive face enter the crematorium,
your hair the first flag to fly
as the door to the bright room opens

and you ride in
looking for your father.

63

The Eyes of Rosenberg

A Poem in One Act

(Muffled bells from St. Andrews Church behind the court house on Foley Square in New York City. As they toll:)

Man A	Man C

batter against the	
	explosion whose
implications	
batter against the	
	explosion whose
	implications
battera	
	batter against the
batter against	
	batter against the

(Both speak at once:)

batter against	institutions
the institutions	of our time
of our time	

(Last bells clang and silence.)

Man A

I come from Julius.

> Woman B *(sings softly
> the Hebrew song, "En Kelohenu"
> while* Man A *continues:)*

Nights in empty airports, rain,
dawn, the wet lips
of Julius Rosenberg, corridors
recovering silence after a day of faces.

Recurrent dreams. I see a
dapper sad-lidded man playing
bad cards. Voices cry "Hide! Change
faces with Proust!" The 2
A.M. departure comes and goes. No flight
is possible for those whose art it is
never to lie.

(Woman B's *singing
trails off.*)

Man A

David Greenglass sharpens
the little points of his smile.

Man C

His A-20 card contains a red dot!

He must have known this either
through direct interrogation by Intel-
ligence officers or via latrine
rumors from "premature anti-
Fascists" interrogated by G-2 on
information received from the
Central Subversive File checks of
the FBI.

Man C
You were scared to death at that time, were you not?

Man A
Yes.

Man C
You have been scared to death ever since, have you not?

Man A
Yes.

Man C
Talk up. Let these people hear you.

Man A
Yes.

Man A

One word, broken, leads to
another, weak links tossed
in a magic box, shaken
and pulled forth a sudden
bright chain to bind
your sister's wrists. Soft
wrists

                             Man C
Did you consult with anybody?

                             Man A
I consulted with memories and voices in my mind.

                             Man C
Did it occur to you at the time, Mr. Greenglass, that
there was a possible death penalty for espionage?

                             Man A
Yes.

                             Man C
You knew that?

                             Man A
I did.

                             Man C
When you said to your wife ''Yes, I will do it'' —
is that correct?

                             Man A
That is correct.

                             Man C
Are you aware that you are smiling?

                             Man A
Not very.

Man C

David,
Little Davie

Woman B *(sings:)*

Uf dem Pripitchickel
Brent a fier-il
in die shtieb is kalt

Zugt shoin nuch a mool
In takke nuch a mool
Kumitz ahliv—ooh

*Sound of teletype, which
becomes a continuing background.*

Zugt shoin nuch a mool
In takke nuch a mool
Kumitz ahliv—ooh

Man A *(overlaps Man C)*

June 15, 1950, to Director:
Urgent: Unknown American number
five, Albuquerque, New Mexico,
Harry Gold dash informant said
photograph resembled unsub, but
that he could not make positive
ident. Gold advised that he
seems to recall that unsub
stated that kosher packages from
New York sent to unsub contained
principally Jewish bread and
salami

Unknown American number five,
Albuquerque, New Mexico, Harry
Gold, informant . . . Kansas City
requests to expedite investi-
gation to locate photo of David
Greenglass, ASN three two eight
eight two four seven three

Your Honor, Gold and Greenglass
were lodged on the eleventh floor
of the Tombs for many months prior
to the trial. There are no separate cells on this floor, which
is reserved for informers; they
are permitted to fraternize without
any restraint by the guards. It is
the section of the jail known as
"Singers' Heaven."

While I cannot take the time
to name all of the men in
the State Department who have
been named as members of the
Communist Party and members of
a spy ring, I have here in my
hand a list of two hundred and
five that were known to the
Secretary of State as being
members of the Communist Party
and who nevertheless are still
working and shaping the policy
of the State Department.

67

Man C

Mr. Gold, I want to interpolate
something at this point. Didn't
you have some recognition sign
as between the two of you?

Man A

Yes, we did, and while this is
not the exact recognition sign
I believe that it involved the
name of a man and was something
on the order of Bob sent me or
Benny sent me or John sent me or
something like that.

Could it have been:
Julius sent me?

(*Sound of teletype abruptly stops.*)

Do you now or
have you ever had a woman
with one brown and one blue eye?
Gold said so and he lied.

Did you not say
as a result of being away . . .?
Gold said so, he told
of his children,

how little Essie broke her leg,
how Dave had polio
but fortunately recovered.
They were lucky. Not to be

born is best. They weren't.
Gold testified and a man
named Rosenberg died—Rosenberg
who had two orphans

in real life.

I come from

Sing

Sing

68

Woman B (*sings*)

Dearest children if I leave you
If the lightning travels through me
If the sunlight burns inside me
Dearest children if I leave you

All day the ward is silent
All day the steel is silent
All day my cell is empty

Pretty babies if they take me
I will watch you from the darkness
You must listen in the darkness
Pretty babies if they take me

All night the ward is silent
All night the steel is silent
All night my cell is empty

(*She stands listening as a distant bell
tolls three times. Then blackout and
instant small spot on* Man A:)

Man A

A deeper commotion, an
inside racket and lights out tell us
the train has entered
a tunnel and is in trouble. Above us
runs a river. Dim blurs
mark the red exit as the noise slows
to a snore of blood going
its final rounds. We have come
to a dead stop. The heart accelerates

in memory of a sign in a room a
lifetime ago: 3 P.M. IS WHEN
                YOUR DAY ENDS.

Man A

It is past supper. We have outlived
our uses. No one speaks.
Small lights hint
in a language too intimate
for our ways
                    red   red

            red

I hear the breathing of invisible men,
invisible women, alive on all sides. Words
swell in the throat, blocking off
breath. I feel
the eyes of Rosenberg
suddenly upon me.
Where is he? In this democracy
of darkness we are
, too close.

(Spotlight begins to dim.)

A final failure
and even the exits are gone. Last color
drains from my eyes. Invisible!
Mouth, hands, invisible! We are
too close. Those troubled, sad-lidded eyes
might be set in my own skull,
though I believe somewhere
above me a mild green world still
waltzes around the sun.

(Blackout.)

En Kelohenu

En Ke-lo-he - nu, en Ka-do-ne - nu,

en K'-mal - ke - nu, en K'mo-shi - e - nu.

Mi che-lo-he - nu, mi cha-do-ne - nu,

mi ch'-mal-ke - nu___ mi ch'-mosh-i - e - nu.

Uf Dem Pripitchickel

Music: A. Warshawsky
(Abridged)

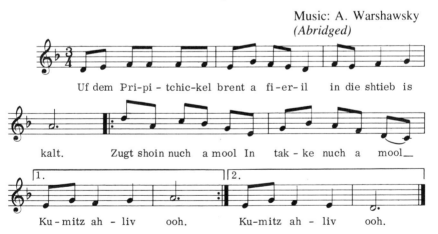

Uf dem Pri-pi - tchic-kel brent a fi-er-il   in die shtieb is

kalt.   Zugt shoin nuch a mool In   tak - ke nuch a   mool___

1. Ku - mitz ah - liv   ooh.   2. Ku-mitz ah - liv   ooh.

Song of Woman B

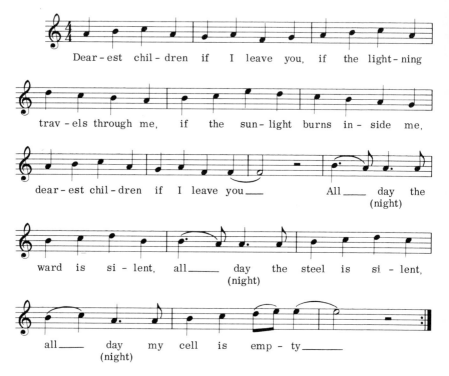

Dear-est chil-dren if I leave you, if the light-ning trav-els through me, if the sun-light burns in-side me, dear-est chil-dren if I leave you___ All___ day the (night) ward is si-lent, all___ day the steel is si-lent, (night) all___ day my cell is emp-ty___ (night)

Pretty babies if they take me
I will watch you from the darkness
You must listen in the darkness
Pretty babies if they take me.

Notes to "The Eyes of Rosenberg": Fewer than half the words in this poem are my own. The opening exchange ("batter against the") originates in the *Columbia Law Review*, February, 1954. Man C's assertions ("His A-20 card" and "He must have known") are in the prose of John Wexley, in *The Judgment of Julius and Ethel Rosenberg* (New York, Cameron and Kahn, 1955). The two exchanges ("You were scared," etc., and "Did you consult," etc.) are from the trial record. The first is from the cross-examination of Max Elitcher, the second from the cross of David Greenglass. The two "Unknown American number five" sections are adapted from FBI documents released to Michael and Robert Meeropol as a result of their suit against the government. The "Your Honor" speech is an adaptation of words spoken in court by Emanuel Bloch, the Rosenbergs' lawyer. The words in the section "While I cannot take the time" were spoken by Joseph McCarthy in Wheeling, West Virginia, February 9, 1950. The exchange with Harry Gold about the "recognition sign" is adapted from pretrial taped interrogations of Gold first made public by Walter and Miriam Schneir in their book, *Invitation to an Inquest* (New York, Doubleday, 1965).

"En Kelohenu" and "Uf dem Pripitchickel" were among the Rosenbergs' favorite songs. Ethel would often sing to herself in prison, and sometimes her voice would carry across the steel and concrete to the cellblock where Julius was kept. The last song (beginning "Dearest children if I leave you") is my own.

IV

The Voice in the Wood

(for Steve Dickman)

There were once three brothers. While they were still quite young one of them, the middle brother, disappeared.

The oldest brother, growing to manhood, would not allow himself to love anyone. Those who cared for him he pushed roughly away. It was the missing brother that he loved and he would not accept his life without him. When his business ventures failed he grew desperate and even contemplated taking his own life.

He decided that it would be best to leave home and to start over in another country. He boarded a ship and set off, abandoning his wife and children and parents.

The youngest brother, meanwhile, was living in a town near the ocean. He could not forget the lost brother either, but as he grew older he allowed himself to love others and to be loved by them. He never believed that his brother was dead, and he continually looked for signs that might lead him to him.

One day he met a man who instructed him to go to a certain place by the ocean and to repeat a certain combination of words. He went to the place, a sandy cove littered with driftwood. As soon as he had uttered the words a great piece of driftwood with much of its bark still attached to it rose up on end before him.

There was a voice in the wood, not words but a resonance, and the sound called forth in the man all his longing for his missing brother.

"Are you my brother?" he said at last.

Something about the wood, the peculiar eloquence of its silence, seemed to confirm that it was, or somehow contained, his brother. By close attention, the man began to understand something of the language of the wood and was able at length to communicate with it.

The wood seemed to beckon the man to the edge of the water.

"I will help you," it said to him.

The man stared into the water and could see nothing; but the spirit in the wood perceived large fish swimming below the surface. Suddenly, to the man's astonishment, the driftwood hurtled into the water with a great splash, changing into a naked man as it did.

In a flash of silver the underwater spirit seized two of the largest fish and threw them out onto the land at his young brother's feet. Once more transforming himself into wood, the spirit rose to the surface and was swept in to the shore by a wave.

The man felt a happiness he had not known since his brother was taken from him many years ago. To be able to speak with him was wonderful, but to have

75

this evidence of his brother's continuing love for him seemed a miracle.

"I will bring these fish home and eat them," he said. "What can I do to repay you?"

"I will tell you," responded the wood. "Wait for me here tomorrow."

At that the driftwood again plunged into the ocean as if hurled by an invisible force. Amid the splash of foam the sunlight glinted for an instant on a wet human thigh.

The spirit of the lost brother swam underwater for hundreds of miles like a silver light. Above him the surface of the ocean was growing choppy, and soon he was entering the region of hurricanes. At last he could see a ship's wooden hull twisting back and forth in heavy seas. He rose to the surface and climbed aboard—a naked young man.

No one noticed him. The sailors and passengers who had not been swept overboard were struggling with the lifeboats or cowering in their cabins. Suddenly the oldest of the three brothers reeled out onto the creaking deck. He was holding a revolver in the air. He stopped and squinted across the rain-twisted expanse at a naked man who seemed the exact image of himself. In his confused mind he imagined he was seeing the beloved brother who had been missing for many years.

The naked man did not speak, but a voice filled the windy distance between them, saying, "You are going to shoot someone. Shoot me."

The oldest brother hesitated, remembering the revolver with which he had intended to take his own life. He leveled the gun at his brother and fired. Immediately, the winds that had been wrenching the ship began to subside.

The next morning the youngest brother was sitting by the shore in the cove of driftwood. A big log with bark still covering one side was suddenly swept in by a wave and deposited at his feet.

"You have come back," said the man.

The wood seemed to speak, saying, "Now you must do the favor you promised me."

"I will do anything. Tell me what it is."

"You must take your knife and destroy me."

The man was astonished at this request.

"Do not be afraid," continued the voice in the wood. "We both will live forever."

So the youngest brother followed the instructions of the voice in the driftwood, and after three days he had carved the wood into a long, slender instrument, hollow in the middle, with a small hole on one side and two sets of three small holes along the other.

He sat down by the ocean and blew softly into one end. A low breathy sound flew forth, full of the resonant voice of the wood.

Istanbul, 1976

76

The Hindu Rope Plant

(for Grace Mostue)

shows its difficulties
leaves twisted
baroquely
as hero's hair
slow strength
delicately raveling
forward
by force
leaves shiny & dark
at the growthpoint
all edges
as if to cut the way
through air
lengthens
over the ebony
tabletop where you
take tea with us
and speak
of Yogananda

Bestiary

K'i-Lin

Gently as a child's kite
the beast stepped from the forest.
In the garden, among
maidenhair trees it found the woman
and knelt
and cast from its mouth
a slip of jade, inscribed:
"The son of the essence of water
shall succeed Chow
and be a throneless king."

Kwei

Between land and heavenly vault,
lower shell and upper, moved
the tortoise, protector
of earthworks, deceiver
of lewd men, slow god.

Out of the waters of the Loh
it stepped and was brought
into the presence of the king.
On its back, in crazed enamel
blotted by age it bore
strange markings.

Fung-Hwang

In the reign of Hwang-ti the first
were seen, male and female
strolling in the eastern garden,
wings gold with dawn.

Millennia later they appeared
in Shantung. A general amnesty
was granted to all prisoners.

Then the last advent. A lone bird
appeared on the tomb of Hung-wu's father,
scratching insane messages
in the dust, its man's eye weeping,
feathers in flames.

Rock	Nude	Sky
		A
phosphorescence	of waves	shattered
smears in the dark	the crest	jewel
among rumors	of leaves	remains
of the once alive	the waved	
	edge	
		the rest
the rest not found	the rest	taken
bundle in	the least	
likely boulders	necessary	
	to perfection	
		the blue
diamonds	the strong	box
can hold	are lightly	tossed
to light	built	in a
		corner
they have		
never known		
	they do	
	not know	
	fear	
		of the
		dark
		room

Song of the Weather

The wind in the trees
           is western,
                  a new slant

on the problem
        of getting the leaves
                      off.

The illogic
      of the approach
               confuses the light

into letting things
           stand
               for themselves.

Look,
you can see them waving.

The Servant

"Matty, here's freedom" — *Emily Dickinson*

To find your freedom behind closed doors
across the open page
into the kitchen, kneeding, setting the bowl
aside in a warm place,
waiting, ramming your knuckles
again and again into the flaccid stuff

going about the house room by room
in the dead of day finding
your freedom behind closed doors
where words
you have often tortured rise to meet you

to take you on
in a terrible silence not even
the slap of letters through the mail slot
can interrupt or the shrieked
annunciations of the telephone

for you have found the self you were
looking for behind closed doors and she
shackles your wrists
to serve no one else and she
extorts from you
at last a sharp sweet savor.

Omelet Vision

(for Joel Oppenheimer)

Cheese and onion omelet
takes form in the young
trucker's mind
above the plastic
menu. Cheese
and onion? repeats
the waitress who thus
joins the dream
in which warm

       slices of onion
      slide over the tongue
   & release
     in a crunch
between teeth their
     sudden savor. Trucker
   nods, leans his head

back into a pungent cushion
of warm cheese.
All over America the bodies
of women
are forgotten in the rush
of steam from mounded plates
lowering
onto countless
counters.

Winning a Poetry Contest

Suddenly it is a day for small errands.
Batteries for the tape recorder, at last
the baby's laughter will be saved.
Waffle-iron fixed after six months
without a transcendant breakfast. The old car
serviced while I stand out in 76
degree April sunlight helping a boy
put a band-aid on a dirty cut.
Finally home to find Libby
bringing in a blazing cake resembling
an unmade bed and inscribed (amid red
sugar roses) "Happy Poetry Rod!"

Pastoral

Beech leaves pressed to paper
under feet
of snow are now released

tan and dried in the May sun
to a tracery
of their former selves.

Against this—twitching off the
    edge of a
grey rock races the world's first

garter snake fluent & green
    jittering
its red tongue.

Pastoral

The snow flies down, the workers
throw up spade after spadeful of dirt
into the yellow truck. The wind flings
the snow to the ground, the workers
bend their backs and toss the dirt
into the truck. Above the town
a crow makes a straight black line
like an accountant.

Istanbul

Gold windows bristling with bracelets,
the shouting merchants: Hey Tall Yes Please!
French sailorboys fresh off the *Clemenceau*
haggling over a bit of red brocade:
"Trop cher!" anger, a threat of blows, a
thousand crowded walkways to help
shake off a pursuing self. Yet it is here,
the vast subterranean city of the grand
bazaar—safe at last—dissolved
suddenly in the exact glance you
stung me with, stranger, standing silent
at the edge of the flowing crowd.
You turned away. The labyrinth was empty.
Bands of stray cats patrolled the darkened walks.

Summer Street

A Poem in One Act

(for Jean)

The four voices in this poem are meant to be heard separately, then conjointly. One must therefore read the poem twice to read it at all, first vertically down the page one column at a time, then horizontally, the eye swinging back and forth across the columned voices.

Notes for performance: Amplified (not too loud) heartbeat fills the dark room. Spotlights on four standing figures:

1. *a female figure wearing a mask indicating a woman of about twenty;*
2. *a female figure, mask indicating a woman of perhaps forty (manner and voice must also convey differences from other woman);*
3. *an "unborn child" figure, perhaps played by a child. This shorter figure wears no mask but is covered with a sheet tied at the neck.*
4. *A male figure, masked.*

Heartbeats continue up to the moment of the child's last words ("with a damp stick"). In the section immediately following that one, the child is present (illumined by pin spotlight) but does not speak. In last two sections child is not present; i.e., spot is out.

2:
She will learn
whose season it is
and around the corners
of what field I have driven
my wooden stakes.
Let her exercise
the prerogatives of perfection,
the black-eyed susan.
The field swells
and she's lost in it.
In her dreams
I have seen to her. I am
summer. I am
beneath her notice.
The way home runs through me
as through the bins
of the dead.

2:
Sizing a grease spot
off black formica
with a dull knife, sweat
sprouting on my brow,
runneling the bones
he once called beautiful,
suddenly the blade
looses a fountain from the
dry hand and I
cry to him, Take her!
Take her deep in the unmown field
where the dew soaks
half her long dress,
and then
Look out: see the massive
head of the beast rise
over the hill like the
tunnel of a black gun

1:                    3:   4:

Think the exact second
talk turned dangerous, her
  back
to the fire, her bare feet
nudging a sleeping dog, it was
no accident, the world tilted
to it as a plane at evening tilts
into a nest of lights: the man
falls into bed with the woman,
stumbles down the wrong street
on a cold night and sees white
chrysanthemums in a yellow
  window,
falls in a trough of leaves
between seasons at the point
of rest between hills

yes,
I am afraid. I need not
one more of your seasons

        is it
        the spurt of roses
not one more overture

        in the
        throbbing bouquet
pounding the ear
from childhood

        thudding
        of toy guns
like the police
saying
Come out singing, I need
not one more

        insomniac
        god
infested civilization
laid on my doorstep
like a carp
to reel me back

        upstairs pacing
        the small room

1:

resolved not to answer

the tug in the wrist . . .
Useless!
    What draws me out
destroys me
    though I rate

down a street strewn
with melon rinds, out

onto the open page
where words stand

like breezeless banners
of heraldry

3:

is it

watery voices

from a garbled war
of annunciations

a great bell

booming in the
darkness

foretelling

the new world

4:

the train, our hands, the rising
    sun

come to grips with what they
    must do
and goodbye. The woods
begin moving north, an old coat
some girl is pulling off, her body

a winter field, her mind a freight
yard outside Trenton.
           I think

of the questions your hand
puts to mine and of the pressure
to perform the part
of crossed lovers forever saying
    farewell
in the shadow of moaning
    machines . . .

4:

Winter passes through the body
of spring into summer. Below cliffs
in shining midnight three figures
compute a stately dance
to seething applause. I pull you in,
woman and woman. Roots
of closely meant trees

seek downwards
till need becomes entangled with desire
and morning comes upon a dream
still struggling in the dirt

1:

words lie slack in the
hands, unhitched

no secrets
to send

blind fingers
reading the ribs

a wet fur coat

distance has done with

heroics of the far flung
simile
like you, like me;

the only connective is

the bum foot

of Oedipus
stumbling to Colonnus

3:

A crystal
of fear in the veins

reaches the unborn

rains

on silver trapezes

swing down the
leaves

to put

out

history

with a damp stick

4:

intermittant signals

like frightened
tympany

interfere with
the sense of loss
necessary to

our love
our upper air ache

over the continental
divide:

1:

My child, my tears
fall in all the wrong places
and will not grow you —

The blue-lined page
buckles under quick droplets,
all wetness lost

and fistless, the line blurs
between life and the jewelry
of your veins,

threaded limbs flung
from the height of the fountain
to a fatal brilliance

3:

1:

the eye rises slowly

along the lines

the long cloud
of her thigh
the first movement

of waking

rises

the sheets fall away

the sun pours in

through the window
of the secret room,

born again

the eye rises
to meet her body
halfway

2:

Above the field

filled with running children
like summer in a bowl

the kites mount

the eyes of the
children rise
along the lines to

a gaudy dissonance

dragons
with fiery tails,
a white ship

the puppetry
of dreams

on slender crosses a child
could break

the kites mount
bearing the name of
summer

into a cooler mass of air—

4:

a slope of air

the snow descending,
a sweep of hands

over piano wires

a laying on of winds

the thought pattern
of glaciers

a mountain,
a room of madness

where memory shatters
the teeth of fossils

1:                          4:

Even the poets
                         Witness, large wet flakes
doubt it, even the poets with catgut and hook
                         overdressed for April commit
in the red dark doubt
                         their beautiful mistake
the movement in the fountain,
                         like charming drunks crashing the wrong party,
Even the lovers
                         Witness, leavelets half
deny what their noses tell them in the rotting springtime
                         unfurling, revolving on twigs like
the sour truth
                         new teeth pulling themselves, pain
when ice trickles and cracks and suddenly
                         in the knuckles of trees
the world starts moving
                         and in the crook
lifting again to the sun sopping ravines
                         Witness, the bright blades flare
and quartz cliffs burn with light
                         as the snow stops and a sun appears
and a shadow moves in the wilderness
                         inside a droplet on a green stem
mountains away